Why God Allows Suffering

Revealing God's Innocence

By Tiger Dragon Storm

Published in 2017 by Heartspace House Publishing

ISBN-13: 978-1-9997677-4-7

ISBN-10: 1999767748

Contents

Introduction

I know it's confusing, if there's a God, why does this God allow suffering?

The reason is this. God, is not a being.

This book speaks from a non-duality/advaita vedanta perspective. The basic meaning of both terms is "not two" "no duality" or "end of knowledge". Implying that literally no two of any-thing exists or ever has or will or even could exist. Also pointing to how knowledge or Mind reaches its "end" or limit through the teaching. Making room for clear un-muddled direct experience to take over in uncovering truth.

The use of the English language in this book may be different to what you're used to. Please re-read sentences or paragraphs if they on first glance seem un-clear to your Mind.

You'll read a lot of "Pure Self" "Awareness" "Pure Consciousness" "Universe" talk that refer to the same thing. Because speaking about God requires a play with language. Also, when I say something is "finite" in this book, I'm saying it from the level of appearances. In other words, as a person speaking to you, the other person, in our "world". Experientially I know that there is only infinite consciousness, and nothing really exists in its own right as a finite object.

A little bit about "me". I had what's known as a "Self-realisation" or "Enlightenment" experience where I saw the "oneness" of all things. Through what I can only describe as "Grace "my perception was shifted allowing me to see the world for what it really is. One undivided immaculate consciousness in different forms. Amongst other realisations I saw what I thought was "my" whole life flash before me and realised "I" don't exist as a separate entity from the all but I am the all and not solely a person!

I found that there is only that which we call "God" or "Source" or "Universe" "Brahman" etc.

We are it, that which cannot be perceived. Hence you can never perceive what is perceiving your thoughts. But you know somehow that the thoughts arise within you...whatever this "you" is.

You've simply been led to believe by thoughts and other people that the thoughts or Mind is a personal object that belongs to an individual "I".

Ironically, after the experience of oneness tones down a little, you come to the realisation that there never was a "person" that had a self-realisation or enlightenment experience. There was and always is just the knowing of experience.

To understand why God allows suffering, which God clearly does, we must first find out if our idea of God is correct. We must begin from the most stable reasonable premise that we can. In other words, we must not rely on imagination to describe what God actually is.

The term "God" is not at all used in the religious sense in this book. The word God has over time become more comfortable for me to use when describing the indescribable since my awakening. So please feel free to change the word in your Mind for "Source" "Universe" or whichever word you feel most comfortable using when describing that which has created the perceived universe.

Now please read on as I explain in more detail about why God allows suffering.

FALSE PREMISE

Holy scriptures and ancient scrolls have been misinterpreted greatly. Talking about God from a false premise. They don't understand that to talk about the unspeakable, imperceivable, that which is *"closer to him than (his) jugular vein", that mysterious one, one must use poetic and subjective language.

This is not at all a dig at religion, it's simply that for some reason the ones given the task of spreading the deep truths of the scriptures, are in no way self-realised. Of course there will be some, but they will be in the tiny minority and wouldn't label themselves "religious" in the first place.

They, the teachers I began speaking of, speak from a place of fear, you must "fear God "for example. This teaching can only be spoken from a person who believes they are separate from God.

For when you know your true essential nature to be that God you seek, fear and any emotion will be recognised for what it is. A simple arising in the Mind with no inherent ill intent. It comes, then goes, but the witness of the coming and going of Mind stays present, and that witness is your true self.

*Quran 50:16

OBJECTLESS GOD

That which we call God is not objective. If God was objective, instantly God would become finite. Which would defeat all understandings of that which we call God being infinite, eternal, who created everything. Something that is finite would have to be created itself in some way. Have a start and end point. Relying on another thing(s) to give it life.

As an example, let's take the religious belief that some prophets have seen or spoken directly to God. In the moment of speaking to, listening to, or seeing God, God would then be within the person's experience. Some inevitable questions the prophets would have pondered if the stories were of real people with understanding in the non-dual reality, would be something like "If I'm perceiving God right now, and my perceptions are known within my Mind, then what proof is there that God exist outside of my Mind? If God can fit into my Mind...then what am I?".

Similarly, many spiritual people will say words to the effect of "God is within", not realising this implies you are greater than God. For how can the creator of all that is, be "inside" you? That makes it objective, "smaller" than you and implies a separation. It's better to be courageous and say that the essential nature of yourself, is God. Although this "oneness" must first be experienced for you to be sincere in your words!

GOD'S EYES

That which we call God is that which allows all experiencing to happen. That which is so close, that you don't need to transcend your body for it. You don't need to hop on a plane to an exotic country to feel the presence more strongly. In fact, there is no place you can go to feel closer to God. Its presence is always here, as it should be, since it's that which we call the almighty God. God cannot be "almighty" if there is any place it cannot be or isn't.

Some religious people will say something like "God could be on Earth but chooses not to be". To say God chose to not be in the world, would just be your belief system setting up its defences on things the Mind can't fathom.

In addition to this, to say God could be in this world, would imply that God is also a finite being, an entity. Naturally speaking, an entity cannot be both finite and infinite, only finite.

God's eyes, are always with you because it is, that, which perceives the "you". Meaning, you have a sense that you exist. Just as you can look at your hand and confirm you are perceiving it. Now pretend your hand is that sense of "I exist" and simply look at it. Do you now see how everything is always known to the witness behind it? Just as you looked at your hand, something is "looking" at your senses.

What evidence is there that a sense has any knowledge of its own existence? Of course if we are to be sincere, the answer would be zero. But what we can say is our collective common experience as humans is, we are all aware of the senses, touch, smell, taste, hearing and seeing. So that which is aware of the senses we know to be the true "I" that perceives experience and is not itself limited to perception or sensation.

This is the same for thought. For what evidence is there that a thought itself can recognise another thought? Again zero. But we can all as people say we are aware when thoughts come and go. That which is aware of thoughts is again the pure "I" knowing that perceives experience whether a thought, sensation or perception.

Confirming that this "I" presence we all share, does not share the limits of thought either as it perceives thought!

Everything is known to a knower so-to-speak. God's eyes, of course I'm using the term "eyes" poetically here, are the reason you can experience anything at all. God's eyes, is the knowing "I".

Furthermore, senses themselves don't have any inherent existence. All there is of so-called "senses" is a sensation or perception. Touch, smell and taste are sensations, hearing and seeing are perceptions. Therefore, senses are a concept that Mind has conceived, as Mind can only perceive by individuating experiences.

GOD & EGO

The source of all "this", we can never get back to. "Why?" You may ask, because we ARE the source.

If that which we call "God" didn't allow for all of experiencing to happen, the good the ugly the bad the suffering the joy. That God would be a being that has its own individual needs, wants, thoughts and preferences like in the religious understanding.

"I like these people but not those people" "these people shine my statues but those do not, so I don't like that" "I think I'll cause a flood now". That's all thought, thought is a limited entity, so the truest idea of God that could not be.

Even if that was your idea of God, one who has choices and wants such as "worship me" or "do these deeds", what would be allowing that God to have those beliefs? Or to exist within experience? Because remember something that is within experience, is experienced itself by something it can never perceive or know. Just as characters in a movie will never be able to perceive you watching the screen, as they are the experience but not the experiencer.

So we see here that God could never be a personal God who has preferences to cause suffering or even joy. For that would make God limited. God being a person is indicative of the limits of Mind trying to understand experience. Mind just throws up a whole lot of thoughts until one thought says "yeah, that makes sense!", although a thought itself cannot know anything. We delve deeper into the illusion of Mind later on in this book.

GOD OR MIND, WHERE DOES KNOWLEDGE COME FROM?

As shocking as this may sound, that which we call God does not know anything per se, as "knowing" is a Mind concept. God just IS all knowledge, just IS all love. just IS the substratum of every experience.

For example, when you want to know what something means what do you do? You pause for a moment and try to think, the Mind slows down until it stops resulting in you not thinking for a second or two, then Mind comes back as the answer.

Do you see what happened? In order for Mind to reform itself as the answer, it had to melt back into itself which is its true nature as the Pure consciousness/God

/Source/Universe or whichever word you wish to conceptualise the infinite as. Mind could only get the answer when it dissolved itself back into God, after the dissolving it was able to re-appear again as the answer.

The funny thing is that it believes it was itself that found the answer...when in fact it wasn't even around when the searching happened!

So, all knowledge is within that which cannot be perceived, in other words God. Yet at the same time, From God's so-called perspective it does not conceptualise anything to be knowledge, all that arises out of it is an activity of itself. You see, knowledge is something to be gained or lost, how can the infinite gain or lose anything? Of course, it cannot, it is already everything. Caricaturing Mind here, the reason Mind believes phenomena such as knowledge can come and go, is because its own experience is of coming and going! This is why we cannot rely on Mind to "reach" ultimate truths.

SAFE FROM SUFFERING

For something to happen there would naturally have to be an allowing for that something to happen. Likewise, for experience to happen there would have to be an allowing for experience to happen.

Walking, talking, thinking, eating, drinking, happiness and suffering everything we experience is known, known by whom or what? What is allowing this very moment to happen? I don't speak of the things or circumstances of the moment, I mean the actual capability of a moment even being possible, what is allowing all this?

To put it another way what is, as is said in many spiritual circles, "holding space" for experiencing to happen? What is that which does not judge, that which has no biases, that which has no wants nor desires. God.

That is what God truly is, it's that imperceivable unknowable-ness that all of "this" is existing within.
Is suffering a pleasant experience? Of course not! We should and do try to cause as little suffering to each other as possible and we should attend to those in need. But is experiencing itself a gift? Of course it is!

That is "God's grace", God's beauty.

The grace/beauty is in the allowing for experiencing to happen at all.

On closer inspection, we understand that if all experience is known and perceived by a subtler part of us, then the experience of suffering for example, is not happening to the essential nature of the pure God consciousness that we are. We, our pure self, is always safely observing the person, rather, the thought of the existence of a tangible person that is within experience from our seat of imperceivable peaceful pure consciousness.

MIND EXPERIMENT

Never try to use your Mind to fathom the unknowable, for Mind itself is finite thus limited. How can one use a limited tool to understand the infinite? It's ludicrous to imagine that could be possible. Mind is beautiful in its apparent own right; hence I use a capital "M" whenever I speak of Mind in this book such is my respect for that which it is. But it is a "middle person" so-to-speak, so not the best tool to discover higher truths. In fact, the attachment to Mind is the very obstacle that obstructs one's awakening.

Mind is an interesting concept, yes Mind is just a concept.

Let's try a simple experiment to find out if that which we call "Mind" actually has a reality of its own. Let us investigate and see if you truly do own a Mind.

But first, moving forwards in this experiment, I hope we can agree that Mind is just a fancy way for saying "thought". There are various definitions of what Mind is but when all is said and done, Mind cannot be separated from thought, for thought is simply what it is.

Mind is seen by many as that which holds all of our personality and memories within.

If this is true, you will now be able to search and find it. In this Mind experiment I now ask you to calmly search for your Mind, your eyes can be opened or closed the choice is up to you.

Have a couple minutes of searching or longer if you so wish, then resume this book from the next paragraph.

Now, did you find it? If your answer was "yes", my follow up question would then be, who is this person saying "yes"? Is that personality not a thought itself? If you are to be honest with your investigation right now your answer will be, yes.

If we are to be sincere with this experiment, otherwise known as "self-enquiry", we discover that it's impossible to find the Mind because Mind is a thought and a thought can not be found by another thought. Because we always experience one thought at a time, there can never be the "I" personality thought meeting another thought to say, "found you!".

Thought is simply that which is known to the desire-less awareness of all experiences. Whether the experience is a simple question from thought, or an earthquake. All experiences you believe you are personally having, are experienced themselves by a subtler part of life that has no personhood itself.

Ultimately, there is no evidence of a personal "you" that owns a Mind. The reason you cannot find the Mind, is because whilst searching for it, the cessation of you being a Mind yourself begins as you melt back into the pure silent sill consciousness that you always are. Because you have shifted your attention back into pure consciousness, the space for a finite object such as Mind cannot be made, as there is no "space" for anything other than pure consciousness. When Mind leaves, you stand alone as pure consciousness.

For Mind to be a container of all of our memories and our personality as is thought in the mainstream view of Mind in the world, Mind would have to be infinite to be constantly recording life. But as we all know experientially, Mind is finite for we are not always thinking, a fact that stands for itself so-to-speak in deep sleep. To say Mind contains memories and personality is imagination, not evidential.

BODY EXPERIMENT

Thoughts will tell you that the body confirms your limited identity as a finite entity. But let's examine this, what do you know of the body? Perception and/or sensation.

Now with your eyes closed, please press your hands together, what are you actually aware of other than the sensation of it?

Of course if you're to be sincere with this experiment, you'll find that "nothing" will inevitably be the answer. You may say "the thought of the sensation" that too would be correct, and prove once again that your only knowledge of a body existing is known within Mind, and as we now know from the previous experiment , Mind does not belong to a personal "me".

Perception or "seeing", is known, thus is also a product of Mind. For something is aware the apparent "seeing" is taking place. We've already discussed how Mind cannot be found when you look for it, so that's seeing gone out the window as a candidate for the proof of a body being your true Self.

As you may have already guessed, this revelation goes for all senses, all senses are known within Mind. Therefore don't actually exist independent of the awareness that they exist in.

NOT TWO

God allows suffering because...God...does not have any biases. From God's "perspective" (I use that term very loosely) it has no concept of right or wrong for that is a play of Mind. God cannot have a belief system. Only something limited could have or even need personal beliefs. That which is Infinite cannot know something personal for that would make it finite.

Imagine a plain black sheet of paper was representing the infinite eternity of existence. You then placed a small round green sticker in the middle, the sticker would have just displaced the infinite space with its own little existence.

Now you have a green dot and the space around it making two things instead of the one. Both would now have a certain dimension to them, an objective quality to distinguish the two.

This is kind of what happens when we perceive as the person aka Mind. We seemingly displace the infinity that we naturally are, and forget we are not a small finite body. The apparent forgetting itself is just a play of consciousness, for consciousness of course cannot "forget" anything.

GOD'S DREAM

Let's live our lives with compassion and love, for those qualities are closest to our nature. Hence it feels horrible to feel or see another in pain. For pain is furthest away from our calm imperturbable peaceful nature.

I want you to really understand and realise that the essence of you is never suffering. You, the truer "you", can never "feel" pain, nor suffering. You are the experiencer of all experiences, just as you experience a movie, but know you're not the characters in the movie. Or experience music playing and know you're the experiencer of the song and not the sounds themselves. You're not the "person" in the experience, as you found out when we did the Mind experiment earlier in this book. The person you think you are that has a personal history, desire and a personality can never be found. All that happens is thoughts arising in the glorious awareness of experience that you truly are.

Just as you cannot find a second ago, or a nanosecond ago, you cannot find this person you believe is you that is suffering, and you never will. Because experience cannot legitimately be attributed to an individual Mind.

Time isn't true, nor is the thought that you're the Mind. Nothing Mind perceives can be happening to you, because Mind itself is an object to a subject, that subject of course being your imperturbable pure self.

The fire and the ocean, the stars and the moon, the pain and the joy, the crying and the laughter all exist within experience. Something is confirming that experiencing is happening, this something must therefore be changeless and unaffected by the experience to allow experience to run smoothly. Even in apparent moments of confusion, there is something coherent enough to confirm the confusion. That experiencer is the true you that is currently experiencing the reading of words.

Hope this helps you and gives you a clearer understanding that from God's so called "perspective" there are no people that are separate from God, for there are no people that are separate from experience. Thus, all people are "inside" God so-to-speak. There is just one big experience, or one big "happening". Only by attaching to Mind do you as Pure consciousness/Source/Universe/God, forget or for all intents and purposes, overlook your nature.

Just as a dream is one big experience of Mind which is thought. Though they may seem separate, both Mind and the waking state are found to be one big experience within God's eternal dream, and you dear reader, are that divine dreamer.

Thank you for taking the time to read this book

-Tiger Dragon Storm

www.ingramcontent.com/pod-product-compliance
Lightning Source LLC
Chambersburg PA
CBHW021121020426
42331CB00004B/577